HOME FOR CHRISTMAS
LEADER GUIDE

Home for Christmas:
Tales of Hope and Second Chances
Leader Guide

Home for Christmas
978-1-5018-7044-6
978-1-5018-7045-3 *eBook*

Home for Christmas: DVD
978-1-5018-7048-4

Home for Christmas: Leader Guide
978-1-5018-7046-0
978-1-5018-7047-7 *eBook*

Home for Christmas: Youth Study Book
978-1-5018-7042-2
978-1-5018-7043-9 *eBook*

HOME FOR CHRISTMAS

LEADER GUIDE

TALES OF HOPE & SECOND CHANCES

JUSTIN COLEMAN

LEADER GUIDE BY SUSAN GROSECLOSE

Abingdon Press / Nashville

Home for Christmas
Tales of Hope and Second Chances
Leader Guide

Copyright © 2018 Abingdon Press
All rights reserved.

978-1-5018-7046-0

Scripture quotations are taken from the Common English Bible, copyright 2011. Used by permission. All rights reserved.

18 19 20 21 22 23 24 25 26 27 — 10 9 8 7 6 5 4 3 2 1
MANUFACTURED IN THE UNITED STATES OF AMERICA

CONTENTS

To the Leader 7

Hope 13

Love 25

Joy 37

Peace 49

TO THE LEADER

"Home for Christmas" is a phrase that evokes images of walking into a warm shelter or safe space, smells of cinnamon and evergreen, and love from family and friends. It evokes feelings of hope, love, joy, and peace. It reminds us of the birth of Jesus. Yet, in this Advent season there are those who do not experience such a home. Rather, there are families who are experiencing deep grief in the loss of a loved one or a vanishing dream; war or violence in their families and communities; the outcomes of systemic discrimination or racism; or poverty and the lack of basic human needs.

These next four weeks, the group will be introduced to Father Gregory Boyle with his wise insights and the transforming work at Homeboy Industries. More than 8,000 former gang members and formerly incarcerated men and women throughout Los Angeles come to Homeboy Industries each year. They are welcomed into a community of mutual kinship and provided a wide variety of services including tattoo removal, anger management classes, and parenting classes. Plus, 200 persons at a time qualify for an 18-month work program that not only hires them for full-time employment but also offers job training and helps them to re-identify themselves, and become contributing members of their community.

In this study, we will focus on the common Advent themes of hope, love, joy, and peace. However, we will explore these themes through the stories of men and women who are a part of Homeboy Industries. Through their relationships and work at Homeboy Industries, they have experienced the hope, love, joy, and peace that God offers through the birth of Jesus Christ. As we study these stories of transformation and the Scriptures, Justin Coleman leads us to a deeper understanding to experience that hope, love, joy, and peace—the new home that God offers all of us. Coleman says:

> I pray you will see that that home is filled with a thrilling hope grounded in the certainty of new life God offers us in Christ. I want you to experience God's tender, steadfast love that always wins out over judgment, and will always offer us another chance, no matter how many times we've failed before. As you read, I hope you will experience the grateful joy of God's love for you, and carry that joy into your relationships with friends, family, and everyone in your community. And by the time you come to the end of this book, I hope that you will have found the full, all-encompassing peace we find in God, the peace that gives us the courage and strength to carry on with confidence, even when it seems nothing is going our way and nothing stays the same. And in all these things, my wish is that you share this home God offers us—especially with those who believe they have no home and no hope. My wish is that you make Advent and Christmas a time to practice this opening of hopeful doors with every person who comes your

way—to do what Christ has done for us. May the hope, love, joy, and peace of Christ be with you. Welcome home!

How to Facilitate This Study

As a group leader, your role is to facilitate the four weekly sessions using

- the book *Home for Christmas* by Justin Coleman
- the *Home for Christmas* DVD
- this Leader Guide

Use these resources to familiarize yourself with the content each week. Read through the corresponding chapter in the book, preview the DVD session, and read through the week's lesson in this Leader Guide.

This guide includes instructions on how to structure a sixty-minute session. Each session opens with a lesson aim, a few themes to develop, a key Scripture, a theological focus, and instructions to prepare for that particular session. Then there are three major movements for each session:

- Building Community (5–10 minutes)
- Going Deeper: DVD, Book, and Scripture (45 minutes)
- Sending Forth Equipped to Serve (5–10 minutes)

Choose the elements from the Leader Guide that you will use each session, including the specific discussion questions. Be prepared, however, to adjust the session as group members interact and as questions arise. Prepare carefully, but allow space for the Holy Spirit to move in and through the group members and through you as facilitator.

HELPFUL HINTS

Preparing for Each Session

- Pray for wisdom and discernment from the Holy Spirit, for you and for each member of the group, as you prepare for the study.
- Prepare the space where the group will meet so that the space will enhance the learning process. Ideally, group members should be seated around a table or in a circle so that all can see one another. Movable chairs are best, so that the group can easily form pairs or small groups for discussion, if your group is large.
- Provide an Advent wreath to use as you close each session. You can purchase one or use a wreath from your home or church. If needed, you can make a simple wreath with a round Styrofoam ring, evergreens, and four purple candles. Plan to have a lighter available each week.
- Ensure that the DVD equipment is set up and working properly.

Shaping the Learning Environment

- Create a climate of openness, encouraging group members to participate as they feel comfortable.
- Remember that some people will jump right in with answers and comments, while others need time to process what is being discussed.
- If you notice that some group members seem never to be able to enter the conversation, ask them if they have thoughts to share. Give everyone a chance to talk, but

keep the conversation moving. Moderate to prevent a few individuals from doing all the talking.

- If no one answers at first during discussions, do not be afraid of silence. Count silently to ten; then say something such as, "Would anyone like to go first?" If no one responds, venture an answer yourself and ask for comments.
- Model openness as you share with the group. Group members will follow your example.
- Encourage multiple answers or responses before moving on.
- Ask, "Why?" or "Why do you believe that?" or "Can you say more about that?" to help continue a discussion and give it greater depth.
- Affirm others' responses with comments such as "Great" or "Thanks" or "Good insight"—especially if it's the first time someone has spoken during the group session.
- Monitor your own contributions. If you are doing most of the talking, back off so that you do not train the group to listen rather than speak up.
- Remember that *you do not have all the answers*. Your job is to keep the discussion going and encourage participation.

Managing the Session

- Honor the time schedule. If a session is running longer than expected, get consensus from the group before continuing beyond the agreed-upon ending time.
- Involve group members in various aspects of the group session, such as saying prayers or reading Scripture.
- Note that the session guides sometimes call for breaking into smaller groups or pairs, if your group is large. This gives everyone a chance to speak and participate fully.

Mix up the groups; don't let the same people pair up for every activity.

- As always in discussions that may involve personal sharing, confidentiality is essential. Group members should never pass along stories that have been shared in the group. Remind the group members at each session: confidentiality is crucial to the success of this group.

HOPE

PLANNING THE SESSION

Lesson Aim

To gain a deeper understanding that our hope is grounded in the certainty that God offers us new life in Jesus Christ and to identify ways that we can support the hopes of others.

Session Themes

Through this session's discussion and activities, participants will be encouraged to

- explore and articulate their understanding of hope;
- explore how those who have experienced life in a gang or incarceration come to find hope through second chances and a new life of possibilities; and
- identify and practice ways to support the hope of others.

Key Scripture

My God, I trust you.
Please don't let me be put to shame!
   Don't let my enemies rejoice over me!
For that matter,
   don't let anyone who hopes in you
     be put to shame;
   instead, let those who are treacherous without
   excuse be put to shame.

Make your ways known to me, Lord;
   teach me your paths.

Psalm 25:2-4

Theological Focus

Reflect for a moment what it means to say that hope is thrilling. It may be thrilling to anticipate the celebration of Jesus' birth through the eyes of a child or grandchild. It may be thrilling to eagerly wait for the arrival of a family member or friend that you haven't seen lately. It may be thrilling to hope for that sense of calm after hectic days of shopping, decorating, baking, and Christmas gatherings. You may have a thrilling moment of awe at the Christmas Eve candlelight service when there is a hushed silence and wonder in the birth of Jesus Christ.

Our thrill of hope is grounded in the certainty of new life that God offers us in Christ. The men and women at Homeboy Industries have found new life in loving relationships and have been given the skills, resources, and encouragement to create a new life for themselves. This newness not only transforms them

14

but also transforms their relationships with others. God through Jesus Christ creates us and claims us. When we trust and live into God's grace and love, we are given the hope of new life that is full of second chances to change and transform our circumstances.

Preparation

- Read and reflect on the Introduction and chapter 1 in *Home for Christmas* by Justin Coleman.
- Preview session 1 on the *Home for Christmas* DVD.
- Read through this session outline in its entirety to familiarize yourself with the material being covered. Be aware that there is a lot of material that can be covered within this session, and your conversations could easily take off and consume much of your group time. Choose the session elements you will use during the group session, including the specific discussion questions you plan to cover. Be prepared, however, to adjust the session as group members interact and as questions arise. Prepare carefully but allow space for the Holy Spirit to move in and through the group members and through you as facilitator.
- Provide a recording of "O Holy Night" and "Come, Thou Long-Expected Jesus."
- Read and reflect on the following Scripture: Psalm 25:1-10.
- Be prepared to read or ask a member of the group to share the story of Jennifer found at the beginning of chapter 1.
- Have an Advent wreath with four purple candles and a lighter.
- Have a markerboard or large sheet of paper available for recording group members' ideas.
- Have a Bible, paper for taking notes, and a pen or pencil available for every participant.

BUILDING COMMUNITY
(5–10 MINUTES)

As participants arrive, welcome them to this study. Depending on how familiar participants are with one another, you might want to spend a few minutes introducing yourselves and sharing why you were interested in doing this study.

In the first session, provide a basic overview of the study and the primary Advent themes of hope, love, joy, and peace. Share with the group that each session will include a conversation starter, a prayer, a video where you will hear from Justin Coleman and persons at Homeboy Industries, a closer look at the book, and an examination of Scripture in light of the week's theme. Tell the group that you will also look for ways to apply what you have learned and to challenge one another to live out the week's Advent theme.

Conversation Starter

Say: One of the lines in the hymn "O Holy Night" is "A thrill of hope—the weary world rejoices."

Ask participants to form pairs and answer the following question: During this Advent and Christmas season, what is the thrill of hope you long for?

Opening Prayer

Play a recording of "O Holy Night," inviting participants to silently reflect on the words, especially ways that Jesus Christ's birth is a thrill of hope.

Pray: *Loving God, in this stillness, we expectantly wait for the birth of the Christ Child. In our weariness, in our brokenness, in our woundedness we wait in hope. We join with the weary world rejoicing in your thrill of hope.*

GOING DEEPER: DVD, BOOK, AND SCRIPTURE (45 MINUTES)

Note: This section allows approximately forty-five minutes for discussion of the DVD, the book, and Scripture. You will not have time to address every discussion question. Select questions in advance that you believe will be most helpful for your group and discuss those questions first. It may help to put a check mark by the questions you want to cover. If time allows, incorporate additional questions.

The DVD

Say: In each week's video, Justin Coleman will share with us the transforming stories of men and women at Homeboy Industries and we will hear Father Gregory Boyle's wise insights. More than 8,000 former gang members and formerly incarcerated men and women throughout Los Angeles come to Homeboy Industries each year. They are welcomed into a community of mutual kinship and provided a wide variety of services including tattoo removal, anger management classes, and parenting classes. Plus, 200 persons at a time qualify for an 18-month work program that not only hires them for full-time employment but also offers job training and helps them to re-identify themselves and become contributing members of their community. Each week, we will explore the week's Advent theme through their stories. As you watch this week's video, consider how persons at Homeboy Industries experience a thrill of hope.

Play session 1 (running time approximately 10 minutes).

Ask: What insights did you gain from the DVD?

The Book

Personal Insights: Invite participants to share sentences or phrases from chapter 1 of Justin Coleman's book *Home for Christmas* that helped them understand hope.

Read aloud or summarize:

Justin Coleman grounds his understanding of hope in God's creation and the Advent of Christ with the possibility of second chances. He says:

> Even when we move away from well-known stories of hope and reconciliation, out into the mess of the real world, my hope is grounded in this new life, this sense of creation and new creation from God. I feel hopeful when I see a child born, knowing it hasn't yet experienced any of the evils of this world, and that it has its whole life ahead of it, ready to grow in surprising ways. I feel hopeful when I see a sprout of new life from a garden, the creation of a beautiful new piece of art, or someone baptized. All new creation. All good. All just what God had in mind. During the Advent and Christmas season, it's not just that we hope Christ will save us or that we hope Christ will return, but that we enter into Christian community expecting new life. Some speak of Advent as a season of generic waiting, as if we were only waiting for Christmas presents or waiting to play Christmas music. But waiting in itself is not quite enough for me. Advent is about waiting with a sense of longing and expectation. We enter into Advent expectantly, trusting that Jesus will come again, and longing for the renewal that Christ brings.

For discussion:

- How have you experienced this cycle of creation and new creation lately?
- What is your hope grounded in?

- What besides the love of God has backed up your hope?
- Describe a time your hope was disappointed. What do you think went wrong?
- Share a time when you were given a second chance and experienced a newness of life.
- What renewal are you hoping that Christ will bring this Advent and Christmas?

Say: Coleman tells us that one of the taglines at Homeboy Industries is "hope has an address." Hear this story of Jennifer, who found hope at Homeboy Industries.

Read aloud or tell the story of Jennifer:

It was the beginning of December, and Jennifer was incarcerated. Separated from her two small children, she spent Christmas facing the possibility of up to thirty-eight years in prison. After agreeing to a plea deal and arranging to live with her mother, Jennifer began working at Homeboy Industries. At first, everything was great; she and her children were making a new life together. But then her mother kicked the entire family out of the house. After such a promising start, Jennifer and her two children were homeless, and she felt like giving up and returning to her past life, and to the drugs and alcohol that had been part of it.

But Homeboy Industries came to Jennifer's assistance, helping her to find a transitional housing program. Able now to pay her rent, Jennifer has started college, and was also able to spend this past Christmas with her children. Not only have the community and support—her new home at Homeboy—given Jennifer this second chance at life, but also she says the love that she finds in and from her new, second family "actually gives me a lot of hope."

For discussion:

- What do you find hopeless in Jennifer's story? What do you find hopeful?

- What makes poverty- or crime-ridden communities easy to dismiss as hopeless?
- Boyle uses a phrase, the " 'no matter whatness' of God." God loves you no matter what, and when you are among the people of God, they are going to love you into newness of life. How were persons at Homeboy Industries an incarnational witness of God's hope to Jennifer?
- Do you think there is a limit to the number of chances we should give people? Why or why not?
- Where are the places or the people in your own community that need to experience God's love no matter what?

Hope in Scripture

In Advance: Use a commentary or Bible dictionary to help you prepare to discuss the Scripture passage. Become familiar with the text. Add questions for discussion that emerge from your study in addition to those below.

Read aloud:

> *I offer my life to you, LORD.*
> > *My God, I trust you.*
> *Please don't let me be put to shame!*
> > *Don't let my enemies rejoice over me!*
> *For that matter,*
> > *don't let anyone who hopes in you*
> > > *be put to shame;*
> > *instead, let those who are treacherous without*
> > *excuse be put to shame.*
>
> *Make your ways known to me, LORD;*
> > *teach me your paths.*

Lead me in your truth—teach it to me—
　　because you are the God who saves me.
　　　I put my hope in you all day long.
LORD, remember your compassion and faithful love—
　　they are forever!
But don't remember the sins of my youth or my wrongdoing.
　　Remember me only according to your faithful love
　　　for the sake of your goodness, LORD.

The LORD. is good and does the right thing;
　　he teaches sinners which way they should go.
God guides the weak to justice,
　　teaching them his way.
All the LORD's paths are loving and faithful
　　for those who keep his covenant and laws.

Psalm 25:1-10

Say: In the first three verses, the psalmist expresses a deep longing and asks God not to put anyone to shame.

For discussion:

- What hopes do you have during this Christmas season in particular?
- Are they any different from the hopes you hold at other times of the year?
- How can we affirm that God loves rather than shames us or our deep longings?

Say: Justin Coleman says of verse 4,

The psalmist is asking the Lord to teach us the paths to God's love and grace that are smooth and that can be navigated without obstruction. As has been the case with many Homeboy

21

participants, we sometimes choose paths that lead us away from God's love and grace—treacherous paths that lead us into hopelessness rather than hope. And when there is no hope, people often wander into life- and soul-threatening situations—drug or alcohol abuse, membership in a gang—as they seek to compensate for or numb their pain. But if the soul can find its way to paths of love and grace, all of a sudden, a new life appears—all of a sudden, there is hope.

For discussion:

- What experiences in your own life have led you away from God's love and grace?
- What experiences in other persons' lives have led them away from God's love and grace?
- How has a path of believing and trusting in God's love and grace led you or others to hope?

Say: In the remaining verses, the psalmist affirms that hope is sustained through our experiences of God's compassion and steadfast love. In the story of Jennifer, the community of love found at Homeboy gives her hope, courage, and joy to fulfill her dreams of a new life.

For discussion:

- Who encourages your hopes and dreams?
- How does someone's support give you courage and joy to work toward your dreams?

SENDING FORTH EQUIPPED TO SERVE (5–10 MINUTES)

Plan to take a few minutes for participants to quietly reflect on what you have discussed during this session. Reflection questions will be provided each week, along with a closing Call to Action, which participants will be invited to receive and engage in between meetings.

Read aloud or summarize:

Part of Homeboy's work involves offering gang members the compassion and faithful love they have never had. Father Boyle talks about young people whose parents or caregivers may only have been there for them in frightening ways. And so, not only did they never experience a calming influence in tense or violent situations; they also learned they could never let their guard down, that it was never safe to accept or offer kindness to anyone, even to oneself—that sometimes, the safest thing to do was hurt others before you got hurt. One of the things Homeboy offers, then, is "attachment repair," learning to be together in—to feel safe in—mutual kinship and support. It's the kind of family Christian communities are called to offer each other, the same kind of mutual vulnerability among its members that allows hope to thrive and new life to emerge.

Reflection Questions: What are you doing in your own faith community to support the hopes of others? What are you doing outside of your community?

Take a few minutes for participants to quietly reflect on these questions and journal their thoughts.

Call to Action

The season of Advent is a time of waiting expectantly and working toward the fulfillment of our hopes and dreams. At the beginning of each day, think about a person you can support in her or his hopes and dreams. It may be something as simple as offering a smile or an encouraging word to a sales clerk who is hoping to finish work or as complex as giving someone a second chance. At the end of the day, reflect on what difference your support might have made in that person's life.

Lighting the Advent Wreath

Read aloud:

> My God, I trust you.
> Please don't let me be put to shame!
> Don't let my enemies rejoice over me!
> For that matter,
> don't let anyone who hopes in you
> be put to shame;
> instead, let those who are treacherous without
> excuse be put to shame.
>
> Make your ways known to me, LORD;
> teach me your paths.
>
> Psalm 25:2-4

Say: As we light this first candle of hope (*light the first candle*), we proclaim that you, O God, are our thrill of hope. You created this world and continue to create and re-create us. Through your love and grace, you give all of us second chances. As we wait expectantly for the birth of Jesus Christ, our hope is thrilled by the suspense of waiting for the surprising ways that you will break through our lives and the lives of others.

Sing together: "Come, Thou Long-Expected Jesus" or another familiar carol.

LOVE

PLANNING THE SESSION

Lesson Aim

To gain a deeper understanding of Christ's transforming love and of ways that we can act with that same love so that our lives and others' lives are transformed.

Session Themes

Through this session's discussion and activities, participants will be encouraged to

- explore and articulate their understanding of Christ's transforming love;
- discover how to be in awe of another person's circumstances and actions rather than being judgmental, thus leading to God's transforming love;
- explore how those who have experienced life in a gang or incarceration come to find a community of love and learn to love themselves and others; and

- practice ways to love others in mutual kinship and with Christ's transformative love.

Key Scripture

This is my prayer: that your love might become even more and more rich with knowledge and all kinds of insight.

Philippians 1:9

Theological Focus

Justin Coleman writes about a transformative love that is open to God's tender, steadfast love. In this love we hold one another accountable for our actions not by hurting another person or being judgmental, but rather by loving one another. Coleman illustrates how Homeboy Industries looks in awe on a person's circumstances and actions as a way to offer God's tender, steadfast love. When we are able to understand and appreciate another person's experience, we are more able to express love for that person rather than being judgmental.

This transformative love is also based on a mutual kinship, where persons stick with each other, hold up one another, and never give up on each other. It seems risky and countercultural to love with tenderness and compassion and to walk with another person in love. However, when we enter into a relationship with another, both lives are transformed. Reflect on the ways you and members of your small group might have been judgmental of another person or a group of persons in your community. Reflect on possible ways to reflect God's tender, steadfast love. Reflect on ways that you have experienced mutual kinship in which both your life and the other person's life have been transformed.

Preparation

- Read and reflect on chapter 2 in *Home for Christmas* by Justin Coleman.
- Preview session 2 on the *Home for Christmas* DVD.
- Read through this session outline in its entirety to familiarize yourself with the material being covered. Be aware that there is a lot of material that can be covered within this session, and your conversations could easily take off and consume much of your group time. Choose the session elements you will use during the group session, including the specific discussion questions you plan to cover. Be prepared, however, to adjust the session as group members interact and as questions arise. Prepare carefully but allow space for the Holy Spirit to move in and through the group members and through you as facilitator.
- Read and reflect on the following Scripture: Philippians 1:3-11.
- Provide a recording of "O Holy Night" and "Love Came Down at Christmas."
- Be prepared or ask a member of the group to tell the story of Carl found at the beginning of chapter 2.
- Have an Advent wreath with four purple candles and a lighter.
- Have a markerboard or large sheet of paper available for recording group members' ideas.
- Have a Bible, paper for taking notes, and a pen or pencil available for every participant.

BUILDING COMMUNITY
(5–10 MINUTES)

Conversation Starter

Say: The third verse in the hymn "O Holy Night" begins, "Truly he taught us to love one another; / His law is love and his gospel is peace."

Ask: What synonyms can you can think of for the word *love*?

Have participants call out these synonyms and record their answers on a large sheet of newsprint or a markerboard. (Ideas: mercy, peace, compassion, friendship, kindness, and so on.)

Ask participants to form pairs and answer the following question: During this Advent and Christmas season, how are you experiencing the love of Christ?

Opening Prayer

Play a recording of "O Holy Night," especially the third verse, inviting participants to silently reflect on the meaning of love expressed in the song.

Pray: *Loving God, we love you with our entire being—with all our heart, all our mind, and all our strength. You show us how to love ourselves and to be a witness of your transforming love. Teach us to love others with mercy, through our friendships and through being kind to others.*

GOING DEEPER: DVD, BOOK, AND SCRIPTURE (45 MINUTES)

Note: This section allows approximately forty-five minutes for discussion of the DVD, the book, and Scripture. You will not have time to address every discussion question. Select questions in advance that you believe will be most helpful for your group and discuss those questions first. It may help to put a check mark by the questions you want to cover. If time allows, incorporate additional questions.

The DVD

Say: As you watch this week's video, consider how persons at Homeboy Industries experience Christ's love and mutual kinship with one another.

Play session 2 (running time approximately 10 minutes).

Ask: What insights did you gain from the DVD?

The Book

Personal Insights: Invite participants to share sentences or phrases from chapter 2 of Justin Coleman's book *Home for Christmas* that helped them understand Christ's transformative love in a deeper way.

Read aloud or summarize:

Justin Coleman states,

> Even though the centrality of love for Christian life seems pretty clear-cut, so does the Christian concern for sin—specifically, for ridding the world of sin. At a couple places where I've worked, we have done major renovations of spaces. Some of those spaces have required an abatement process to create a safe environment for workers and those who would eventually inhabit those spaces. I'm always impressed by the fact that the Church is in the sin-abatement business. We work to diminish sin and the effects of sin in the lives of those who believe.

And so the Church talks about ways to remove the effects of sin from the world—about the best way to carry out the sin-abatement business. There are at least a couple of approaches to this work that the Church might take. One is to judge or discipline sin's effects out of this world. This posture says that if we discipline people—if we judge between what is good and bad or right and wrong in the life of an individual or community, then we might offer enough of a corrective that the individual and/or community would become free of sin's effects. This position is like a bloodhound tracking down sin—always seeking to sniff sin out. When this sin is found, the bloodhound bites in and doesn't let go until it gets the result it wants.

Trying to judge sin out of the world is not meant to be a malicious activity. This kind of practice is meant to act as a form of accountability, or a discipline that leads to righteousness. But the Church can so easily wound people. My experience is that Christians tend to carry this idea that God sent that inflection of God's self that is the Son into the world to right wrongs—particularly the wrong of sin. To a certain degree this is true. Jesus' ministry does involve setting aright wrong thinking and actions so that the wrong can be made right or made new. But sometimes we are so fixed on being right and pointing out wrongdoing that we miss the mark of the high call of God in Jesus Christ to love the sin out of the world.

For discussion:

- How have you experienced the Church as being in the sin-abatement business? How has it been negative? How has it been positive?
- Think of a time you were judged by another person. What feelings did you experience?

30

- What does it mean to "love the sin out of the world"?
- Father Boyle at Homeboy suggests that we are to be in awe of another person's burdens rather than judging how they carry them. What would happen if you stood in awe of the burdens a person carries, instead of judging how she or he is carrying them?
- Do you think acting out of love instead of judgment is especially important as we move toward Christmas? Why or why not?

Ask: How would you define Christ's transforming love?

Write the group's ideas on a large sheet of newsprint or a markerboard.

Say: Justin Coleman describes Christ's transforming love as a tender kindness in which persons stick with each other, hold each other up until they're whole, and never give up on one another.

For discussion:

- When have you experienced Christ's transforming love as a tender kindness? Have you witnessed people sticking with each other, holding each other up until all were whole? Have you received love that did not give up on you?
- Are there any particular places or people in your community in need of this transforming love?
- How can you act with a tender, steadfast love that transforms those places and/or lives?
- We often hear something described as "a Christmas miracle." When do we expect transformative love to act with the speed of a miracle, providing instant, predictable results?

Love in Scripture

In Advance: Use a commentary or Bible dictionary to help you prepare to discuss the Scripture passage. Become familiar with the text. Add questions for discussion that emerge from your study in addition to those below.

Read aloud:

> *I thank my God every time I mention you in my prayers. I'm thankful for all of you every time I pray, and it's always a prayer full of joy. I'm glad because of the way you have been my partners in the ministry of the gospel from the time you first believed it until now. I'm sure about this: the one who started a good work in you will stay with you to complete the job by the day of Christ Jesus. I have good reason to think this way about all of you because I keep you in my heart. You are all my partners in God's grace, both during my time in prison and in the defense and support of the gospel. God is my witness that I feel affection for all of you with the compassion of Christ Jesus.*
>
> *This is my prayer: that your love might become even more and more rich with knowledge and all kinds of insight. I pray this so that you will be able to decide what really matters and so you will be sincere and blameless on the day of Christ. I pray that you will then be filled with the fruit of righteousness, which comes from Jesus Christ, in order to give glory and praise to God.*
>
> Philippians 1:3-11

Read aloud or summarize:

Jesus also demonstrated to us what love looks like. Jesus taught us how to love one another by loving us. His loving example was caught as much as it was taught, meaning that his disciples witnessed in him the kind of love that he preached.

The Apostle Paul reminds us what Jesus' demonstration of love looked like in Paul's letter to the Philippians. The third verse of the first chapter begins with thanksgiving. It begins with Paul reminding those he is addressing in the church of Philippi just how much they mean to him—he's reminding them that their souls have worth. Now, a thank-you does not give you your worth. Your worth is already there. But a thank-you *does* serve to remind you of how much of a difference you make in the lives of those who have offered thanks.

After he gives thanks to the Philippians, in verse 9, Paul shifts his thoughts to prayer. The apostle's prayer is for love to be perfected. He writes them in the hopes that their "love might become even more and more rich with knowledge and all kinds of insight." It is a prayer for the growth of the beloved community—not just in terms of numbers, but also in terms of the depth of their transformative love for each other, their ability and commitment to be steadfast in their tender interaction with one another. It is growth into what we call "holiness" in my church tradition: the perfect love of God and neighbor.

Activity: Paul expresses how much he loves the church of Philippi by naming what he is grateful for and his prayers for the church. Create two lists. On the first list, name why you are grateful for your church. On the second, name the prayers for your church.

For discussion:

- Review the two lists. How does your church express Christ's transforming love? Where is your church growing in its love for others?
- How does learning to love others require learning to love yourself? How might understanding Christ's love help us do this?

- Dr. Martin Luther King Jr. envisioned a beloved community where love transforms enemies or opposers into friends. Where have you experienced such a beloved community?
- What does the growth of the beloved community mean to you? What does it mean for your church?

SENDING FORTH EQUIPPED TO SERVE (5–10 MINUTES)

As you close each week's session, plan to take a few minutes for participants to quietly reflect on what you have discussed during the session. Reflection questions will be provided each week, along with a closing Call to Action, which participants will be invited to receive and engage in between meetings.

Read aloud or tell the story of Carl:

Carl admits that the atmosphere at Homeboy Industries might be a little disorienting to visitors, who are probably used to seeing tattoos and thinking, "Gangs! Danger!" Visitors may expect the homeboys and homegirls to give them "some type of look" demanding to know why they're there—may expect anything but the loving welcome they receive when they walk through the doors. Carl says it's the evident kinship at Homeboy that helped him learn how to communicate with other people—and how to love both them and himself. "That's love for me," he says: the fact that this place has brought together onetime enemies and turned them into family.

Read aloud or summarize:

And speaking of Carl, Homeboy has been a place that has even allowed him to be less of an enemy to himself. And able now to recognize the pain of his past life in a gang, he is able to live with the continuing repercussions of his personal history—wounds that include being unable to walk and being confined to a wheelchair—without allowing that past to define or limit him or his ability to love. "I really learned how to communicate my feelings. I learned how to love myself and I'm no longer living that selfish lifestyle that I once did. I come into these doors every day and I receive so much love. I wake up every day wanting to be here," he says.

You probably know someone like Carl, someone in need of tenderness, in need of the steadfast kindness that God offers us. My prayer is that we will learn the lessons of love that Christ is trying to teach us, and that this love—this tender, loving kindness—will be the law of our hearts and the guiding spirit behind all of our actions.

Reflection Questions: During this Advent season, who needs to experience this tender, loving kindness? How can you show Christ's transforming love to that person this week?

Take a few minutes for participants to quietly reflect on these questions and journal their thoughts.

Call to Action

Read 1 Corinthians 13 at least once a day this week. See what parts of it speak most strongly to you and look for opportunities to put the chapter's words into practice (with yourself, with your family, in your community, and/or with Jesus Christ).

Lighting the Advent Wreath

Read aloud:

This is my prayer: that your love might become even more and more rich with knowledge and all kinds of insight.

Philippians 1:9

35

Say: As we light this first candle of hope (*light the first candle*), we are thrilled by the surprising ways that Christ will break through our lives and the lives of others. As we light this second candle of love (*light the second candle*), we commit to loving ourselves and others with Christ's transforming love.

Sing together: "Love Came Down at Christmas" or another familiar carol.

JOY

PLANNING THE SESSION

Lesson Aim

To gain a deeper understanding of God's gift of joy and ways that we can share this gift of joy, especially by standing with people who dwell in lowly places.

Session Themes

Through this session's discussion and activities, participants will be encouraged to

- explore different meanings of the word *joy*;
- explore how those who have experienced life in a gang or incarceration come to find a community of love where they can experience the joy of reconciliation; and
- practice ways to share God's gift of joy by standing with people who dwell in lowly places.

Key Scripture

> The LORD your God is in your midst—a warrior bringing victory.
>
> He will create calm with his love;
> he will rejoice over you with singing.
>
> *Zephaniah 3:17*

Theological Focus

When was the last time you experienced joy? How do you experience joy in the times of life that are exciting and full of happiness? How do you experience joy even at times of struggle, chaos, or uncertainty? How might those who live in lowly places of poverty, discrimination, racism, abuse, and violence come to experience God's joy?

Zephaniah reminds us that God rejoices in us, and that this joy allows us to rejoice in each other, to support one another, and to be there for each other. In this session, we will explore the Hebrew word *simcha*, which means a complete joy or an assurance of God's faithful, abiding presence. We will reflect on this understanding of joy in our own lives as well as in relation to persons who may not experience such joy.

Challenge the group to explore ways this Advent and Christmas to rejoice over others just as God rejoices in us. Challenge the group to identify ways that they can walk with another in this season who might not know or trust in God's *simcha*. Experience the grateful joy of God's love for you and lead the group to carry that joy into their relationships with friends, family, and everyone in your community.

Preparation

- Read and reflect on chapter 3 in *Home for Christmas* by Justin Coleman.
- Preview session 3 on the *Home for Christmas* DVD.
- Read through this session outline in its entirety to familiarize yourself with the material being covered. Be aware that there is a lot of material that can be covered within this session, and your conversations could easily take off and consume much of your group time. Choose the session elements you will use during the group session, including the specific discussion questions you plan to cover. Be prepared, however, to adjust the session as group members interact and as questions arise. Prepare carefully but allow space for the Holy Spirit to move in and through the group members and through you as facilitator.
- Read and reflect on Zephaniah 3:14-20 and prepare the index cards for the word study.
- Provide a recording of "O Holy Night" and "Joy to the World."
- Be prepared or ask a member of the group to tell the story of Theo found at the beginning of chapter 3.
- Have an Advent wreath with four purple candles and a lighter.
- Have a markerboard or large sheet of paper available for recording group members' ideas.
- Have a Bible, paper for taking notes, and a pen or pencil available for every participant.

BUILDING COMMUNITY
(5–10 MINUTES)

Conversation Starter

Say: Verse one of the hymn "O Holy Night" says that "the weary world rejoices" at the birth of Christ. Joy is central to rejoicing.

Ask participants to form pairs and answer the following questions: What does joy mean to you? How are you experiencing joy this Advent?

Opening Prayer

Play a recording of "O Holy Night," inviting participants to silently reflect on the meaning of joy expressed in the song.

Pray: *We join with Mary, Joseph, the angels, shepherds, and wise ones rejoicing in the birth of the Christ Child, Jesus. This Christmas, may we receive the gift of joy knowing with assurance that Christ is our Savior and that Christ is always with us.*

GOING DEEPER: DVD, BOOK, AND SCRIPTURE (45 MINUTES)

Note: This section allows approximately forty-five minutes for discussion of the DVD, the book, and Scripture. You will not have time to address every discussion question. Select questions in advance that you believe will be most helpful for your group and discuss those questions first. It may help to put a check mark by the questions you want to cover. If time allows, incorporate additional questions.

The DVD

Say: As you watch this week's video, consider how persons at Homeboy Industries experience God's joy.

Play session 3 (running time approximately 10 minutes).

Ask: What insights did you gain from the DVD?

The Book

Personal Insights: Invite participants to share sentences or phrases from Justin Coleman's book *Home for Christmas* that helped them understand joy in a deeper way.

Read aloud or tell the story of Theo:

Before he got involved with Homeboy Industries, Theo felt trapped in a negative environment. Using drugs, spending most of his time in the street with gang members, he says he was "heartbroken." But as Father Gregory Boyle and the staff at Homeboy began offering him support and assistance, Theo says he began "opening up his eyes." He was astounded that people from outside his neighborhood were willing not only to welcome and help him but also to provide more support than any people he'd known before. In this place where the doors are never closed to anyone, Theo experiences "a feeling of joy" being around onetime enemies who now "are just a single family"—who, he says, "look out for one another."

For discussion:

- What did Theo need to experience joy in his life?
- Coleman subtitles the story of Theo "The Joy of Reconciliation." How is reconciliation a source for one's joy?
- What are ways that you are family to one another in your congregation? How are you family to your community?

Read aloud or summarize:

When we rejoice over one another—when we delight in one another—we are, in a sense, offering the joy we have to the other person. We are re-joy-ing. We are regifting a joy that was given to us. And this gifting and regifting of joy never diminishes the quality of the joy.

As you might have guessed, this joy has a lot to do with love. I talked in the last chapter about loving sin out of the world instead of trying to eradicate it through judgment—through what we might want to call the removal of joy. Let's bring that steadfast, tender love back into the picture and look at how regifting the joy we've been given is often shown by giving—gifting—a second chance to people.

For discussion:

- When have you experienced a second chance in life? When have you given another person a second chance in life?
- When you gift another person with a second chance, how does that person experience joy? How do you experience joy?
- How might you experience regifting the joy that was given to you through Jesus Christ?
- Do you think it's necessary to experience love in order to experience joy? Why or why not?
- Coleman shares stories of persons experiencing a fear of loss that keeps them from fully experiencing joy or complete contentment. When have you experienced a fear of loss?
- Do you remember any time when everyone in a group or community experienced joy? What about that experience made it joyful for everyone?

Joy in Scripture

In Advance: Use a commentary or Bible dictionary to help you prepare to discuss the Scripture passage. Become familiar with the text. Specifically explore verse 17 (The LORD your God is in your midst—a warrior bringing victory. / He will create calm with his love; / he will rejoice over you with singing.) in a commentary and add questions to enhance your study.

You will need five index cards. On each card write one of these Hebrew words—*GILA, RINA, DITZA, HANAAH,* and *SIMCHA.* If possible, provide a dictionary of Hebrew words.

Read aloud:

> *Rejoice, Daughter Zion! Shout, Israel!*
> > *Rejoice and exult with all your heart, Daughter Jerusalem.*
> *The LORD has removed your judgment;*
> > *he has turned away your enemy.*
> *The LORD, the king of Israel, is in your midst;*
> > *you will no longer fear evil.*
> *On that day, it will be said to Jerusalem:*
> > *Don't fear, Zion.*
> > *Don't let your hands fall.*
> *The LORD your God is in your midst—a warrior bringing victory.*
> > *He will create calm with his love;*
> > *he will rejoice over you with singing.*
>
> > *I will remove from you those worried about the appointed feasts.*
> > *They have been a burden for her, a reproach.*

Watch what I am about to do to all your oppressors at
that time.

I will deliver the lame;

I will gather the outcast.

I will change their shame into praise and fame
throughout the earth.

At that time, I will bring all of you back,

at the time when I gather you.

I will give you fame and praise among all the
neighboring peoples

when I restore your possessions and you can see
them—says the LORD.

Zephaniah 3:14-20

Word Study

Say: Zephaniah 3:17 says that God rejoices over us. The Hebrew
language has different words and meanings for the word *joy*.

Divide the class into five small groups. Give each small group
an index card with one of the Hebrew words written on it.

Say: Reread the section "The Joy of Christ" in Coleman's
book *Home for Christmas*, paying close attention to Coleman's
description of the Hebrew word written on your group's card. If
possible, look up the word in the Hebrew dictionary and read the
definition and/or description. Be prepared to share the meaning of
your word with the larger group.

After the groups have had time to study the words, have them
share their insights with the larger group.

For discussion:

- How have you experienced *gila* in your own life? *rina?*
  ditza? hanaah?

- How have you experienced God's *simcha*—complete joy? How would you describe this type of joy?
- Zephaniah says God "will rejoice over you with singing." What does it mean that God rejoices over us?

Read aloud or summarize:

Coleman further uses the hymn "Blessed Assurance" to describe God's *simcha*. He says,

> The possibility of having joy, then, is hard for some of us to open ourselves up to until we realize that joy is not the same as happiness. Joy is not a feeling to be conjured up that then remains vulnerable to being taken away in a moment; joy is an assurance....
>
> There is something unique about knowing that you are in Christ. That Christ is in your heart. That Christ is your savior, and that in that way, Christ is yours. It's assurance. Assurance is a confidence in what you have. "Blessed Assurance" has always seemed a joyful hymn to me because the joy comes from assurance in Christ. Here we see that joy is something that we have because it has been given.

For discussion:

- What are ways that you experience joy as an assurance rather than just happiness?
- What are ways that we can offer joy to persons who do not know God's assurance or do not experience joy?
- Is there any special way in which the Christmas season is joyful for you? What makes it unlike the joy you find during other times of the year?
- Why do you think some people, even those who have lives we think of as successful, have such a hard time finding joy at Christmas? How can we help people find joy at Christmastime in particular?

SENDING FORTH EQUIPPED TO SERVE (5–10 MINUTES)

As you close each week's session, plan to take a few minutes for participants to quietly reflect on what you have discussed during this session. Reflection questions will be provided each week, along with a closing Call to Action, which participants will be invited to receive and engage in between meetings.

Read aloud or summarize:

In Los Angeles and beyond, Homeboy has given participants the ability not to "be anxious about anything," because they've found the joy of kinship, of knowing that they're supported, of experiencing "the peace of God that will keep their hearts and minds safe in Christ Jesus."

And the joy isn't just in being safe and loved; Father Gregory Boyle says that this joy is rooted in what he calls "being in companionship with Jesus." This companionship is summed up by St. Ignatius's call to "see Jesus standing in the lowly place."

Reflection Questions: How might you stand with people dwelling in lowly places? How do you think standing with persons in lowly places will bring them joy? How will it bring you joy?

Take a few minutes for participants to quietly reflect on these questions and journal their thoughts.

Call to Action

As we move closer to Christmas, our hearts are full of joy as we anticipate the joy of Christ's birth. We also find joy as we excitedly await being with family and friends. See how many ways you can share your joy of the season with other people, especially those who are dwelling in lowly places.

Lighting the Advent Wreath

Read aloud:

> *Be glad in the Lord always! Again I say, be glad! Let your gentleness show in your treatment of all people. The Lord is near. Don't be anxious about anything; rather, bring up all of your requests to God in your prayers and petitions, along with giving thanks. Then the peace of God that exceeds all understanding will keep your hearts and minds safe in Christ Jesus.*
>
> *Philippians 4:4-7*

Say: As we light this first candle of hope (*light the first candle*), we are thrilled by the surprising ways that Christ will break through our lives and the lives of others. As we light this second candle of love (*light the second candle*), we commit to loving ourselves and others with Christ's transforming love. As we light this third candle of joy (*light the third candle*), we experience the joy of living together in the kinship of Jesus Christ.

Sing together: "Joy to the World" or another familiar carol.

Session 4

PEACE

PLANNING THE SESSION

Lesson Aim

To gain a deeper understanding of peace as God's *shalom* and of ways that we can experience Christ's peace in our lives.

Session Themes

Through this session's discussion and activities, participants will be encouraged to

- define and understand God's peace as *shalom*;
- explore how those who have experienced life in a gang or incarceration come to find Christ's peace at Homeboy Industries; and
- practice developing kinship relationships that promote justice so that we all know and experience God's *shalom*.

49

Key Scriptures

*He will stand and shepherd his flock in the strength of
the* LORD,

> *in the majesty of the name of the* LORD *his God.*
> *They will dwell secure,*
> *because he will surely become great throughout the
> earth;*
> *he will become one of peace.*

Micah 5:4-5a

He has shown strength with his arm.

> *He has scattered those with arrogant thoughts
> and proud inclinations.*
> *He has pulled the powerful down from their thrones
> and lifted up the lowly.*
> *He has filled the hungry with good things
> and sent the rich away empty-handed.*

Luke 1:51-53

Theological Focus

As you conclude this session, the group discussions use the insights from the previous three sessions to gain a deeper understanding of peace. God's *shalom* or peace is more than the absence of war, violence, or chaos. God's shalom is all encompassing. It is a complete wholeness knowing that no matter what happens in our lives, God is our source of hope, God's love is steadfast, God has a constant joy in us and all of humanity, and we are part of God's lasting peace that cannot be destroyed. God's shalom gives us the courage and strength to be confident, even when it seems nothing is going our way and when nothing stays the same.

Our experience of God's *shalom* is rooted in relationships that foster kinship and promote justice. Explore together how the birth of Jesus Christ and his ministry on earth demonstrates God's *shalom*. Encourage and challenge the group to not only identify persons who are experiencing injustices but to consider ways that they can foster loving, supportive relationships and kinship. Explore specific ways that members of the group can not only act with love and kindness but also work for justice so that all experience God's *shalom*.

Preparation

- Read and reflect on chapter 4 in *Home for Christmas* by Justin Coleman.
- Preview session 4 on the *Home for Christmas* DVD.
- Read through this session outline in its entirety to familiarize yourself with the material being covered. Be aware that there is a lot of material that can be covered within this session, and your conversations could easily take off and consume much of your group time. Choose the session elements you will use during the group session, including the specific discussion questions you plan to cover. Be prepared, however, to adjust the session as group members interact and as questions arise. Prepare carefully but allow space for the Holy Spirit to move in and through the group members and through you as facilitator.
- Prepare four sheets of paper or a markerboard with the headings HOPE, LOVE, JOY, and PEACE for discussion of the book.
- Read and reflect on the following Scriptures: Micah 5:2-5 and Luke 1:46-55.

- Provide a recording of "O Holy Night" and "Star-Child."
- Be prepared or ask a member of the group to tell the story of Christina found at the beginning of chapter 4.
- Have an Advent wreath with four purple candles and a lighter.
- Have a markerboard or large sheet of paper available for recording group members' ideas.
- Have a Bible, paper for taking notes, and a pen or pencil available for every participant.

BUILDING COMMUNITY
(5–10 MINUTES)

Conversation Starter

Say: One of the verses in the hymn "O Holy Night" says:

Truly he taught us to love one another;
His law is love and his gospel is peace.
Chains shall he break, for the slave is our brother,
And in his name all oppression shall cease.

Ask participants to form pairs and answer the following question: What does Christ's peace mean to you?

Opening Prayer ((*Psalm*)3)

Invite participants to sit comfortably with their feet on the floor and their palms facing up on their laps. Invite persons to set aside in their mind any distractions and worries. Together take a few deep breaths.

Pray: *God of peace, in this stillness, we place ourselves in your loving hands asking you to slow us down. We release the chaos of this extremely busy season—all the things that exhaust us—knowing that you are always with us no matter what is stirring and churning in our lives. We release into your care any problem or issue that we are facing, trusting in your wisdom and goodness. We release ourselves into your transforming love and seek your justice wherever there is war, violence, discrimination, and injustice. Calm our spirits. Fill us with your peace.*

Play a recording of "O Holy Night" as participants silently experience the gift of peace that is found in the birth of Jesus Christ.

Say: All God's people said, **Amen**.

GOING DEEPER: DVD, BOOK, AND SCRIPTURE (45 MINUTES)

Note: This section allows approximately forty-five minutes for discussion of the DVD, the book, and Scripture. You will not have time to address every discussion question. Select questions in advance that you believe will be most helpful for your group and discuss those questions first. It may help to put a check mark by the questions you want to cover. If time allows, incorporate additional questions.

The DVD

Say: As you watch this week's video, consider how persons at Homeboy Industries experience the gift of Christ's peace.

Play session 4 (running time approximately 10 minutes).

Ask: What insights did you gain from the DVD?

The Book

In Advance: Hang up four large sheets of newsprint or divide a markerboard into four columns. At the top of each sheet or column write one of these words—*HOPE, LOVE, JOY*, and *PEACE*.

Read aloud or summarize:

As we conclude this study,

> Let's take a step back and look at where we've been, what we've learned about God's gifts that are made present at Advent. We said in [session] 1 that the hope God offers us is grounded in reality, that it gives us reason to look with thrilling anticipation to what's to come. And we said next that God's tender love is steadfast, that it sticks with us even when we feel like we've used up all of our second chances. And finally, we learned that God rejoices in us, and that this joy allows us to rejoice in each other, to support and be there for one another.

Ask: Thinking back on our time together and our discussions, what key insights from the first three sessions have been the most meaningful for you?

Write down the key words and/or phrases that the group shares under the appropriate headings on the newsprint or markerboard.

Say: Today we explore further our understanding of Christ's peace.

Personal Insights: Invite participants to share sentences or phrases from Justin Coleman's book *Home for Christmas* that helped them to understand peace. Add key words or phrases to the list under the PEACE heading.

Say: The Hebrew word for peace is *shalom*. As Justin Coleman explains,

> God's *shalom* is all encompassing. It's the peace of all things. Complete wellness. Wholeness. The wholeness of knowing God's grounded hope, steadfast love, and constant joy in us and in other people. It's the wholeness that goes beyond mere circumstance, the wholeness that allows us to live in the confident knowledge that no matter what happens on a daily basis, we are part of a lasting peace that cannot be destroyed.

For discussion:

- How have you experienced God's complete peace or *shalom*?
- Coleman says that at times we experience peace, but it is short-lived, and stress and chaos quickly return. What sorts of circumstantial peace have you relied on in your own life? Describe the disappointment you experienced when these moments of peace didn't last.
- Do you know a person who seems to have found lasting peace? How do you see peace revealed in that person?

Read aloud or summarize:

Justin Coleman writes,

> Father Gregory Boyle has a saying: "No kinship, no peace. No kinship, no justice." But on the other hand, if there is kinship, we will know justice. If there is kinship, we will know peace. It seems I'm complicating the issue again! What does this mean, this link between peace and justice and kinship?
>
> Simply this: that where there is kinship, we live into our baptismal vows. Where there is the kinship born of God's peace, we resist evil, injustice, and oppression in whatever

forms they present themselves, because that evil is preying upon our kin. Because in God's peace, everything is all good, we work to see that good in the world, striving to achieve the wholeness there that we've received in Christ.

You see this resistance-through-kinship at Homeboy Industries. The changes this place works in participants' lives don't just stay within its walls. One area of focus at Homeboy has been on changing thoughts within the larger society about how we deal with those who have committed crimes. Father Boyle has emphasized that instead of simply locking people up, we need to look at what's driving them to commit crimes—and then to address those causes, such as poverty and lack of opportunity. For example, Father Boyle notes that most of the problem in his part of Los Angeles is a lack of jobs, and Homeboy works to provide those jobs. But the organization also realizes that just finding people employment won't solve lasting emotional trauma that often impairs job seekers' efforts to be successful. For young people who haven't developed the relational skills and trust necessary for attachment that most of us take for granted, building such skills is essential to keeping the jobs they've found. And so Homeboy offers services such as counseling that will help these young people to heal. It's a way of repairing harm—of restoring some justice to an unjust situation, of bringing peace into lives that have known no peace—that has influenced the way in which not only Los Angeles, but other cities around the world as well, have approached criminal justice. Homeboy's work has convinced police to replace "the 'tough on crime' mantra that predominated in the 1980s and 1990s with a 'smart on crime' model" that aims to reduce crime through understanding and addressing the needs of underserved populations. It has convinced even law enforcement—a group often seen as working against the interests of certain populations—to try and reduce instances of injustice where they find them.

For discussion:

- How do you experience kinship in your own relationships?
- How do you develop this kinship with persons who find themselves on the margins of society?
- What is the difference between acts of love or kindness and acts of justice?
- What are ways that you act for justice?
- Do you think kinship is necessary for there to be justice? Why or why not?
- What injustice in your community could you address? How can you develop a kinship in working against this injustice?
- How do you experience God's *shalom* through relationships of mutual kinship? Through relationships that promote justice?

Peace in Scripture

In Advance: Use a commentary or Bible dictionary to help you prepare to discuss the Scripture passages. Become familiar with the text. Add questions for discussion that emerge from your study in addition to those below.

Read aloud:

As for you, Bethlehem of Ephrathah,
    though you are the least significant of Judah's forces,
        one who is to be a ruler in Israel on my behalf
        will come out from you.
    His origin is from remote times, from ancient days.
Therefore, he will give them up
    until the time when she who is in labor gives birth.
    The rest of his kin will return to the people of Israel.

He will stand and shepherd his flock in the strength of
the LORD,

    in the majesty of the name of the LORD his God.

    They will dwell secure,

    because he will surely become great throughout the
    earth;

    he will become one of peace.

Micah 5:2-5a

For discussion:

- How do you describe the gift of peace found in the birth of Jesus Christ?
- How do you understand the kinship of Israel from which Jesus was born?

Read aloud:

Mary said,

    "With all my heart I glorify the Lord!

       In the depths of who I am I rejoice in God my
       savior.

    He has looked with favor on the low status of his
    servant.

       Look! From now on, everyone will consider me
       highly favored

          because the mighty one has done great things
          for me.

    Holy is his name.

       He shows mercy to everyone,

          from one generation to the next,

          who honors him as God.

He has shown strength with his arm.
He has scattered those with arrogant thoughts
and proud inclinations.
He has pulled the powerful down from their
thrones
and lifted up the lowly.
He has filled the hungry with good things
and sent the rich away empty-handed.
He has come to the aid of his servant Israel,
remembering his mercy,
just as he promised to our ancestors,
to Abraham and to Abraham's descendants
forever."

Luke 1:46-55

For discussion:

- How do you understand the gift of peace found in the birth of Jesus Christ as described in Mary's song?
- How significant is the relationship or kinship that Mary has with God?
- What kinship does Mary proclaim will be created through Jesus' life?
- What key words or phrases describe Jesus' work for justice?
- How can you work to bring justice and peace into people's lives?

SENDING FORTH EQUIPPED TO SERVE (5–10 MINUTES)

As you close this week's session, plan to take a few minutes for participants to quietly reflect on what you have discussed during this session. A reflection question is provided, along with a closing Call to Action, which participants will be invited to receive and engage in during the coming week.

Read aloud or tell the story of Christina:

Before Christina came to Homeboy Industries, she was having a hard time on her own—with the big things, like getting sober and finishing school, and even with the things that should have been easy, like spending time with her daughter. But Homeboy has been helping to make things less stressful for her, providing Christina with tools to help her focus, to form relationships, to live the life she wants to live. One of the things she values about the therapy sessions and the classes Homeboy offers her is the fact that, as she says, "everyone is going through the exact same thing you are going through. It feels so good to have that support." She credits the organization with helping her work toward her high school diploma, and toward becoming a drug and alcohol counselor. And even more importantly, Homeboy has given her the peace "to be present" with her daughter. Because of this loving home of strangers who have become a family, Christina has also found the peace that has enabled her to make a new, loving home with the family she's always had.

Read aloud or summarize:

Father Gregory Boyle says, "Sometimes you have to reach in and dismantle messages of shame and disgrace that get in the way so that the soul can feel its worth." This dismantling is precisely what God set in motion at Christmas, precisely what we celebrate and anticipate during Advent: God having reached into the world in Jesus Christ to undo these narratives and their power over us, to give us a new home and new stories about who we are and were created to be, for ourselves and for each other. God reached into the world to replace these lies with divine hope, with grounded hope that can thrill in the certainty of its fulfillment. God replaced this hurt with the steadfast, tender love that never lets go, no matter how many chances we've already had. God replaced these false messages with the joy taken in us, God's creatures, and with the joy we take in each other. And God replaced our doubts about ourselves with the peace of knowing that God's hope, love, and joy will last, no matter what the issues are that we face or the changes that are taking place around us. God reached into the world through Jesus to do all of this.

Ask: As you have seen and heard the stories of men and women at Homeboy Industries, how have they experienced a dismantling of shame and disgrace to experience a new home in Christ?

Read aloud or summarize:

If you know kinship, you will know peace, and you will know and work for the justice that flows from this divine gift.

My challenge to you is that as you see injustice in the world, seek relationship with those who are being marginalized. Know and be known, and may that knowing bring God's shalom into your lives.

Reflection Question: Are there any particular types of injustice you or your family should address as we move toward Christmas?

Take a few minutes for participants to quietly reflect on this question and journal their thoughts.

Call to Action

This week identify and list the people in your community who are experiencing injustice. List the places you see the need for justice in your community.

Decide on at least one way you can develop a kinship and work together toward justice for a person or situation in your community this week. Follow through on your plan.

Afterward, reflect on the way(s) you experienced the gift of Christ's peace. How might others have experienced this gift?

Lighting the Advent Wreath

Read aloud:

> *She gave birth to her firstborn child, a son, wrapped him snugly, and laid him in a manger, because there was no place for them in the guestroom.*
>
> *Nearby shepherds were living in the fields, guarding their sheep at night. The Lord's angel stood before them, the Lord's glory shone around them, and they were terrified.*
>
> *The angel said, "Don't be afraid! Look! I bring good news to you—wonderful, joyous news for all people. Your savior is born today in David's city. He is Christ the Lord. This is a sign for you: you will find a newborn baby wrapped snugly and lying in a manger." Suddenly a great assembly of the heavenly forces was with the angel praising God. They said, "Glory to God in heaven, and on earth peace among those whom he favors."*
>
> Luke 2:7-14

Say: As we light this first candle of hope (*light the first candle*), we are thrilled by the surprising ways that Christ will break through our lives and the lives of others. As we light this second candle of love (*light the second candle*), we commit to loving ourselves and others with Christ's transforming love. As we light this third candle of joy (*light the third candle*), we experience the joy of living together in the kinship of Jesus Christ. As we light this fourth candle of peace (*light the fourth candle*), we know that the birth of Jesus Christ brings to all persons God's hope, love, and joy that last forever, no matter the challenges and changes in our lives.

Sing together: "Star-Child" or another familiar carol.